WHITTLING

Devised and drawn

by

ROSALIE BROWN

Published for

CHIP CLUB

by

JOHN GOODCHILD, PUBLISHERS

70 CARRINGTON CRESCENT, WENDOVER, BUCKINGHAMSHIRE

TELEPHONE: WENDOVER (0296) 623646

First published May 1977

Also by Rosalie Brown

COVER DESIGN AND ILLUSTRATIONS BY ROSALIE BROWN

© ROSALIE BROWN 1977

ISBN 0 903445 47 6

PRINTED IN GREAT BRITAIN BY
R. J. ACFORD LTD.,
CHICHESTER, SUSSEX

CONTENTS

FOREWORD

Whittling is a very simple form of woodcarving. It is a craft probably as old as the first man who used a flint tool.

It is not a difficult craft to master. With only a sharp penknife, practise – and patience – it is possible for anyone to achieve beautiful work, from the very simple to the highly decorated.

This book is intended to be an introduction to Whittling. As well as practical information, it contains a number of ideas to try. Remember, though, that a great part of the immense satisfaction which you will get from whittling comes from turning the nondescript piece of wood in your hands into a creation of your own design.

Rosalie V Brown

CHAPTER ONE

Tools and equipment

The tools and equipment you will need for whittling are listed below. Because it is important to have the right equipment, each item will be discussed briefly before we go on to the actual whittling.

1. Penknife
2. Oil-stone and light oil; carborundum or whetstone
3. Leather strop
4. Emery-paper on a board, or a grindstone
5. Sandpaper: fine, medium and coarse grades
6. Hacksaw
7. Finishers
8. Rags.

PENKNIFE

The best knife to use is a strong, light penknife with, at most, two blades of different sizes made of fine steel. (fig. 1a) Knives which have everything from a corkscrew to a button-hook are far too bulky to hold in comfort for any length of time, and all too often have blades of inferior quality steel.

Fig. 1a

A fine blade like that of a craft knife is not suitable for normal whittling, but it can be useful when doing the fine detail in complicated work.

Sheath knives vary considerably in quality, from the very good to the very inferior. If you have one, keep it for coarse work such as the removal of large amounts of unwanted wood.

OIL-STONE/CARBORUNDUM

A blunt knife is a dangerous knife. Instead of cutting into the wood, a blunt blade will slide or skid across the surface and might cut you. So keep your knife sharp at all times, using either an oil-stone or a carborundum. For advice on the correct use of these stones see **Sharpening a penknife** on page 7.

LEATHER STROP

Use this for putting a keen finishing touch to the sharpened edge of the blade, and also for removing any burr which may be on the edge. (Burr is waste steel turned up by the sharpening action.)

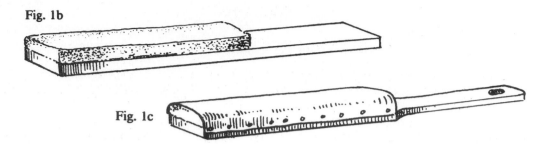

Fig. 1b

Fig. 1c

If you do not want to buy one, you can make your own strop quite easily. Glue a piece of plastic foam to the flat surface of a strip of wood. (fig. 1b). Over the foam place a strip of strong leather, such as calf-leather, and nail it to the wood along the sides. (fig. 1c). Smooth the handle until it is comfortable and easy to hold.

EMERY BOARD

Not many people have grindstones with which to restore a chipped knife-edge. A good substitute is a piece of emery-paper glued to a strip of wood. It is also more useful if you are working away from home. (fig. 1d).

Fig. 1d

SANDPAPER

You will need this to help in the shaping of your wood, and also to achieve a smooth surface for the final finish. Smaller pieces are easier to use, so cut up the sheet if it is large. Examples of fine grades are: flour; 'O' and 'OO'.

HACKSAW

This is useful for cutting wood to the right size for the contemplated work, and for trimming roughly to shape.

FINISHERS

These are not essential if you prefer to leave the wood in its natural state. But you can use linseed oil, ordinary wax polishes, paint, stains and varnish for finishing off.

Painted work needs protection, and White Spirit Varnish is the best to use. Don't be tempted to use any old varnish which you might find in your garden shed; it just won't do. Varnishes are made for specific uses. Some colour the wood; some are slow drying. It is safer to stick to White Spirit and be sure of the result. It can be bought in small bottles from Art shops.

CHAPTER TWO

Sharpening a Penknife

As has been pointed out already, it is unnecessarily risky to try whittling with a blunt knife. So, before you start, inspect the blade of your penknife. Hold the knife sideways (fig. 2a); if the cutting edge is jagged, then it must be put into working order again.

This is when a grindstone is useful. Drop a little water on the stone. Lay the blade lightly against it, and gently turn the stone **towards** the knife edge, moving the blade from side to side with an even pressure so that the wheel grinds the whole length of the blade. Turn the knife over and repeat the process on the other side. Alternate the action until the chipped part has been ground away. (fig. 2b). Wipe the blade.

If you do not have a grindstone, you must use your emery board. Hold it firmly, and lay the blade flat on it. Lift the back of the blade slightly off the board, and, again, with even pressure, move the blade, but this time move it **backwards**. This will prevent the knife cutting the emery cloth. Turn the blade as before, and continue the operation until the chip has disappeared. Moving the blade in an oval pattern will prevent excessive wear in one place. (fig. 2c). Wipe the blade.

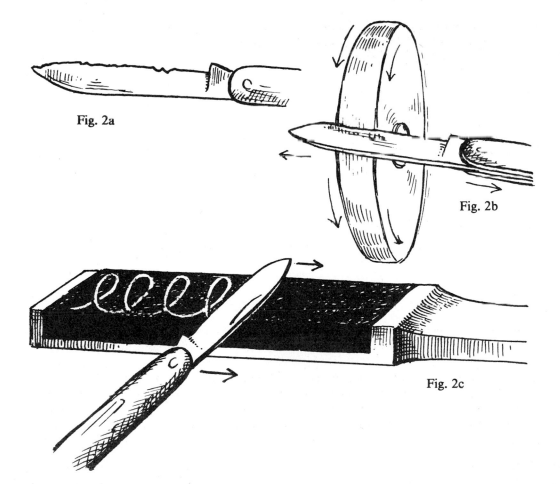

Fig. 2a

Fig. 2b

Fig. 2c

If your blade is very badly chipped, you will have to use a grindstone. That may mean taking the knife to your local ironmonger if you cannot otherwise get the use of a grindstone.

Once your blade is free of chips, you can start the sharpening process. Put a little oil on the oil-stone, and place the blade flat on it. Raise the back slightly, and move it both **forwards** and **up and down** in a circular movement, so that the whole of the blade comes into contact with the stone. Use the whole length of the stone to avoid wearing it away only in the centre. (fig. 2d, e). Turn the blade over from time to time so that it does not become too worn on one side. Wipe the blade.

Testing for sharpness

Stand in a good light. Hold the blade, with the newly-sharpened edge uppermost, and look along the edge. If you can see a reflection from the extreme edge – it will look like a thin white line – then it is not really sharp enough and will require further working on the oil-stone. The absence of a reflection means that the edge is too fine to reflect light, and it must, therefore, be sharp. (Truly a case of: 'If you can't see it, it's there!') (fig. 2f).

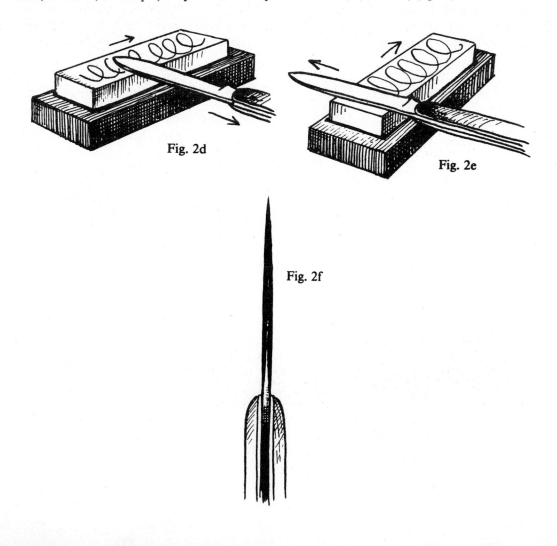

Fig. 2d

Fig. 2e

Fig. 2f

If parts of the edge reflect light, then concentrate on just those parts until the line disappears completely. Remember to wipe the blade and stone after use.

To finish the sharpening process, the blade should be drawn backwards across the strop to remove any burr remaining. Both sides of the blade need this treatment. Remember to draw the blade **backwards**; if you move it forwards, you will end up having to make a new strop!

To test for sharpness, try cutting a piece of paper. If it cuts when you apply only very slight pressure, then it should be sharp enough to do the work expected of it. If, instead, it drags the paper, or merely scores it, then it is certainly not sharp enough for wood. You will find that good quality steel will take, and keep, an edge for longer than poor steel. So, investing in a good quality steel knife will pay dividends in the long run if only by saving you a lot of time in tool care and maintenance.

Once your knife is in good working order it is easy to keep it so if the blade is gently stroked on the oil-stone immediately you feel it drag, slip or slide on the wood. Some woods are harder than others and will dull the blade of your knife quicker. You will soon recognise those woods, and you must be prepared, in your own interests, to retouch the blade quite often. You should **never** take risks with a knife, so obey the rule to sharpen the blade immediately it starts to drag.

Make a habit of wiping the blade immediately after any contact with a sharpening device. Work nearing completion can be spoilt by oil from the stone, or emery dust.

CHAPTER THREE

Woods, and how to identify them

Before you choose a piece of wood to start whittling, it is a help to know some of the properties of the different woods to be found. Most types of wood can be used for whittling, but some are better than others. Those illustrated here are the most commonly found in any neighbourhood.

To help you, each tree is presented in both its summer and winter forms, with its leaves, buds and seeds or cones alongside. There is also a list of the trees, with a description of the wood, its workability and its commercial uses. It is useful to know if the wood you are about to use is suitable for the project you have in mind. For example, it is not much use making cutlery from resinous wood – unless you like the flavour of resin added to your food! So the descriptions include notes on the wood's hardness or softness, whether it is knotty or smooth, and whether it is resinous or not.

When you are in the country, or even a local garden, keep your eyes open for branches brought down by the wind, or left behind after tree fellers have been at work. The best wood is that which has been broken off and left hanging in the tree for some time, because this will have been seasoned naturally. Wood that has been lying on the ground for some time is likely to be rotten or infested, so it is not very useful.

Be careful about sticks you may see in hedges, as they may have been inserted purposely to strengthen the hedge. As a general rule, leave hedges alone.

Build up your own store of sticks. If they are left for a while before you use them they will have seasoned a little and will be much better to use.

A useful source of wood is kindling bought from a wood merchant. The main drawback is that such wood is usually rather short for most objects, but you can use it for small animals, short paper-knives, buttons or toggles.

The wood found in most homes – cigar boxes; date boxes; old packing cases, picture frames and furniture – is excellent material as it has been well seasoned. Their thinness limits the usefulness of cigar and date boxes, but as you will see on page 39, there are some things for which that type of wood is ideal.

Driftwood from the sea shore or the banks of a fast-flowing river is also usable, but it must be thoroughly dried off before carving.

If you live in a city, and you find it difficult to get hold of wood, your local woodmerchant will probably be happy to let you have off-cuts. And you can, of course, buy off-cuts from any 'Do-it-yourself' shop.

When you are whittling a branch, you will notice that the wood nearest the bark, the sapwood, is lighter in colour than the wood in the centre, which is the heartwood. The sapwood is that part of the tree that carries nourishment to the rest; it is much softer, and takes longer to season. The heartwood, on the other hand, no longer carries sap; it seasons better, and is harder than the sapwood.

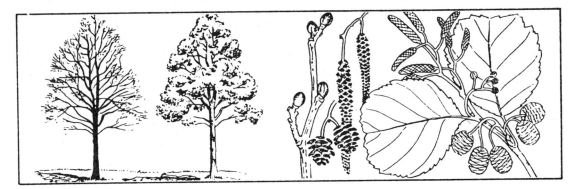

ALDER: Smooth, fine grain, soft wood. Whitish-yellow, turning slightly pink when seasoned, and often flecked by the ravages of insects, which can add to its attractiveness. Used for carving; cabinet work; bridge foundations; piers; toys; pencils. Good to work.

ASH. Tough, pliable, smooth. Yellowish to greyish white, or even pale brown. Used for oars; axe and hammer shafts; archery bows; wheelspokes; fences. Good to work.

BEECH: A straight-grained hard wood. Whitish yellow, or pale brown with a reddish tinge in time. Used for furniture; tool handles; parquetry; thin boxes. Easy to work.

11

BIRCH: Hard, strong and close-grained. Yellowish white, often with small brown flecking due to insect infestation. Used for turnery; packing cases; walking sticks; canoes. Good to work.

ELDER: The new wood is soft, the branches with pith, not heartwood. Old wood is very hard and strong. Yellowish white. Used for engravings; toys; skewers. Excellent for spoons.

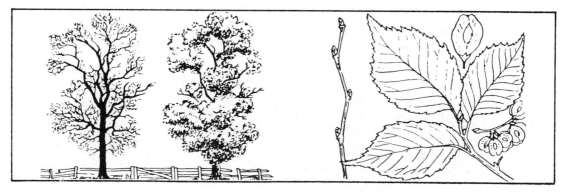

ELM: Hard, tough; fine grain, sometimes twisted. Light in colour. Stands up well to water. Used for water troughs; water wheels; pumps; boats; furniture.

HAWTHORN: Dense, hard wood; fine grain. Light yellow in colour. Used for carvings; tool handles; walking sticks; mallets. Good to work.

HAZEL: Soft but tough and pliable. White or reddish. Used for walking sticks; thatching rods; divining rods. Easy to work.

HORSE CHESTNUT: Soft but tough. Cross grained. No distinct heartwood. White. Used for kitchen tables and utensils; hat blocks; racks for fruit storage.

LIME: Soft, silky, close grain. Whitish yellow. Used for fine carvings (especially by the famous woodcarver, Grinling Gibbons); musical instruments; furniture; kitchen utensils. Good to work.

MAPLE: Hard, and fine textured. White, greyish or pale brown. Used by cabinet makers for choice work: turnery; bowls; spoons. Polishes well. Good to work.

OAK: Hard, tough, strong. Yellowish light brown. Used in ship and house building; carvings; panelling; furniture. Cuts clean but hard.

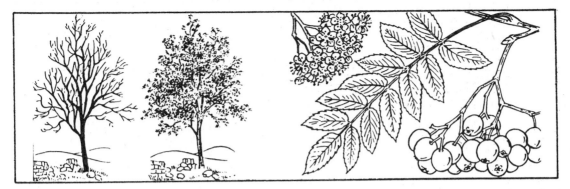

ROWAN: Sometimes known as **Mountain Ash.** Hard, pliable, smooth, dense fine grain. Light reddish to brown. Used for turnery; carving; cabinet work; tool handles; farm implements. Good to work.

SYCAMORE: Hard, strong, firm, fine, silky grain. White to yellowish. Used by cabinet makers for gun stocks; musical instruments; veneers; parquetry. Easy to work.

EVERGREENS — **Do not shed their leaves**

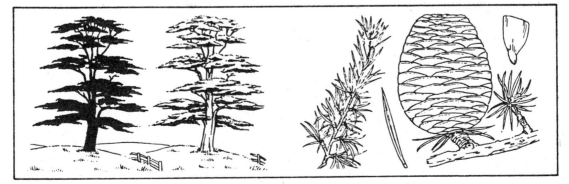

CEDAR: Soft but tough. Lovely colouring from light cream to pinkish brown. Sweet scented. Extensively used for clothes chests and closets. Good to work.

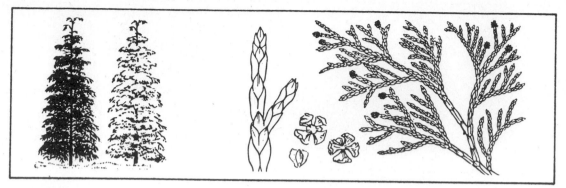

CYPRESS: Close grain, light brown in colour. Scented. Resinous. Used in joinery; fences; clothes cupboards and chests. Easy to work.

DOUGLAS FIR: Straight grained, coarse, knotty but strong. Yellowish white to reddish brown. Resinous. Used for ships' masts; spars; ladder poles; house and ship fitments; pit props; bridge foundations; joinery. Soft to use.

SCOTS PINE: Fairly hard and strong, not too knotty. Yellowish white. Used for buildings; poles; pitprops; fences; telegraph poles. Easy to work.

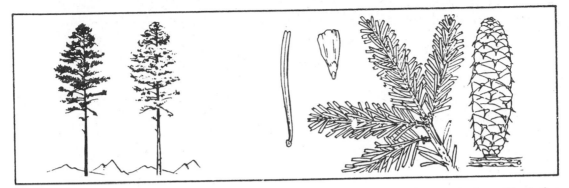

SILVER FIR: Soft, pliable, irregular grain. Greyish white. Resin-free. Used for carpentry; inside of furniture; boxes.

SPRUCE: Tough, pliable, even fine grain. Light whitish yellow. Used for picture frames; ladders; masts; oars; violin and cello fronts; kitchen tables and dressers Fairly easy to work.

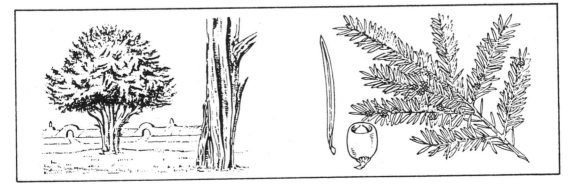

YEW: Strong, tough, pliable, fine textured and hard. Yellowish white to a golden brown. Resin-free. Used for ornamental carvings; bowls; cabinet work; archery bows.

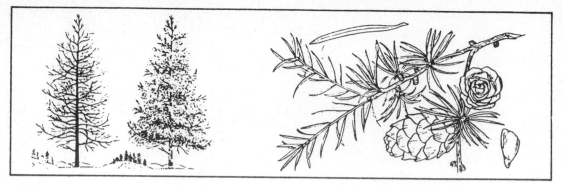

LARCH:
This is not an evergreen, but it is included with them because its wood is rather similar. In appearance, too, it looks like an evergreen, with its long, narrow leaves. Its wood is coarse in texture, strong and hard. Yellowish white. Resinous. Used for telegraph poles; masts; props; planks. Can be difficult to work.

'Knots' in wood are formed where a smaller branch has left the larger. They can be very hard to whittle away, and as several of the woods listed above can be knotty, you should exercise care over the choice of each piece of wood.

The above is not a definitive list of the trees you can find in Britain. There are many, many more whose wood is suitable for whittling. You will be able to identify them by reference to your local library.

CHAPTER FOUR

First steps: paper-knives

When you have sharpened your knife to your satisfaction, you are now ready to try your skill. Make a few practice cuts on spare wood to get the feel of the knife. Start with small chips, making them larger and deeper as you gain full control over the knife. With small cuts you will be able to take off just the right amount of wood. Deeper cuts require more skill if you are to avoid splitting the wood or cutting deeper than you intended, which could leave a notch marring what was intended to be a smooth finish. The simple answer to this problem is to avoid deep cuts whenever possible. Even with the removal of large areas of wood it is better to use small cuts and patience.

Do remember to cut **away** from you as much as you can. (fig. 4a). Hold your arms close to your body, thus getting more leverage and better control over the blade. It is also a less tiring position for working.

When it is necessary to cut towards you, position the thumb and fingers of the hand holding the wood **behind** the blade. Or, if you are working on the end of the wood, keep your thumb **below** the work. (fig. 4b).

The thumb of the hand not holding the knife can be used to push gently on the back of the blade, which will give you more control when you are doing fine work. (fig. 4c).

If you find it necessary to whittle downwards, rest the wood on a firm surface. Try to use a board or an old table; if you use a stone or iron surface, a slip of the knife could result in a chipped blade which will require hard work to repair. It is possible to work with a board on your knees, but if you do, take extreme care if you are using strong pressure; if the board slips, the result will be cut clothing or flesh. (fig. 4d).

You may well find that your hands get tired quite quickly at first. Don't try to carry on if they do. Tiredness can end in less control over the knife, which in turn can lead to mistakes. Instead, rest your hands for a while. You will find that in time, you will be able to work for longer and longer periods as your hands become accustomed to the work.

Your index finger will be doing most of the work, and it will, therefore, be liable to blister. Protect it with a piece of sticking plaster. An injured finger can also reduce your control over the knife, and you could ruin work nearing completion, thus possibly wasting hours of careful whittling.

When you feel you have practised enough, start on a simple, but effective, piece to carve. A paper-knife is just such a piece; it is fairly easy to do, and has a practical use, even if inexpertly carved, when it has been completed.

Paper-knife

If you are going to whittle anything other than an ornamental carving, start by deciding exactly what function the piece should perform. A paper-knife is used to cut paper, usually

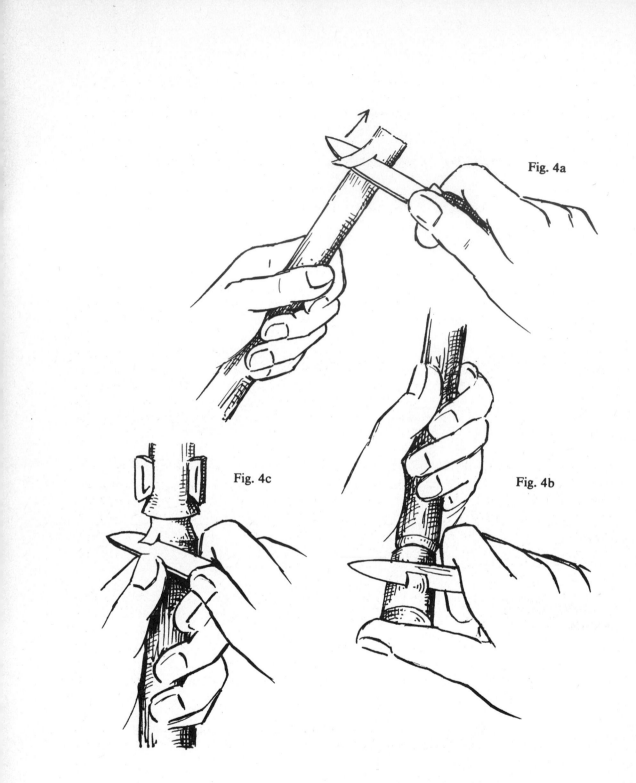

Fig. 4a

Fig. 4c

Fig. 4b

along a folded edge – such as the top of an envelope. The knife should, therefore, be long and tapering, and fairly sharp along at least one of its edges. The end which will be held in the hand when the knife is in use must be comfortable to hold, and free of any sharp edges.

These are the points to bear in mind when you are selecting a suitable piece of wood.

You could start with a small branch, but it should be no thinner than your thumb. Or you could choose a flat, lathlike strip of wood. The first will require more whittling than the second, and, at the halfway stage, will resemble it. So, to cover both possibilities, we will start with a small branch.

A length of from 20–30 cms (8–10 ins.) is adequate. Don't be impatient and start hacking away at the top, where it is being held. Start at the bottom end, and whittle small cuts, working backwards to the hand holding the work. (fig. 4e & f). Remember that you want a flat blade for your paper-knife, so don't allow the stick to turn while you are cutting.

When you have passed the halfway mark along the stick, turn it top to bottom and start whittling from the bottom again. Carry on until you have a piece of wood flat and level on one side, and rounded on the other. The piece must then be turned over so that the process can be repeated on the new side. (fig. 4g.). Do nothing about the edges at this stage; just concentrate on achieving a flat, smooth piece of wood of even thickness throughout its length. (fig. 4h).

The next stage is to decide which end of the piece is to be the handle and which the blade. (Whilst coming to a decision, it might be a good idea to take the opportunity to resharpen your knife.) When you have made your decision, hold the handle end of the paper-knife, and start whittling away at the bottom, keeping in your mind's eye the eventual shape of the object. Moving slowly backwards with each cut, thin down one edge until the work has the shape illustrated in fig. 4i. It should taper in thickness from one end to the other, and also across the blade so that the cutting edge is thinner than the back.

As an alternative, you could taper the blade from its centre out to each edge, making each edge a cutter. This is slightly more difficult, but it can be rather more effective. (fig. 4 IV h).

A common mistake made by many new whittlers is to try and finish off one part first and then move on to the next. Instead, you should bring along the whole of the carving at the same time, turning the work constantly until the whole form emerges, before you start putting the finishing touches.

Fig. 4i shows the blade thinned down to a cutting edge, and the tip shaped to a suitable point. The handle part is thicker than the blade, so the whole piece thins down from one end to the other.

Leave the blade portion alone when it requires only finishing, and concentrate on the handle part. First, decide the particular shape or design you wish to have. Then, start working, resting your hand quite frequently because this work can be more tricky than the blade and you will need to keep complete control over your penknife.

Board

Fig. 4d

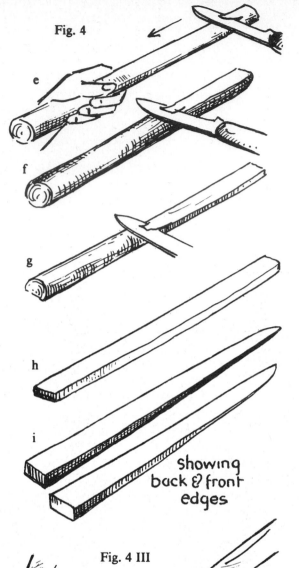

Fig. 4

e

f

g

h

i

showing
back & front
edges

Fig. 4

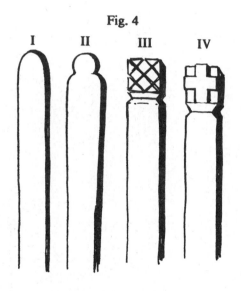

I   II   III   IV

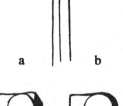

Fig. 4 II

a   b

c   d

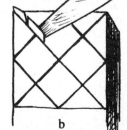

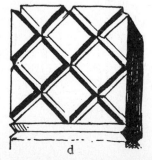

Fig. 4 III

a   b

c   d

22

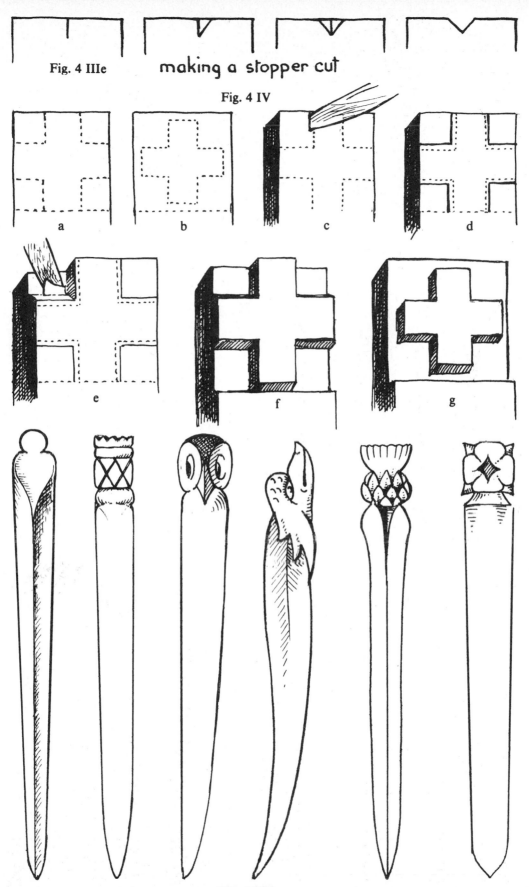

Fig. 4 IIIe

making a stopper cut

Fig. 4 IV

a

b

c

d

e

f

g

Fig. 4 IV h

23

Fig. 4—I: The easiest shape to achieve is to rub down the corners with a coarse grade of sandpaper, and smooth off with a fine one. A design, or your initials, can be painted on to the flat surface, and the whole handle varnished.

Fig. 4—II: On one side draw a simple outline, like that illustrated. Make a small cut in one corner, across the grain. (fig. 4—IIa). From the top, make another cut to meet it, removing a small chip from the whole side. A further slice can then be taken from each side of the cut already made, starting always across the grain, and bringing the other cut down to it. This technique avoids splitting the wood. Continue these small slices until the outline is almost reached. You must take care here to cut evenly through the thickness of the wood, so that the back and the front are the same. Pare off the corners, and then sandpaper to the final shape. (fig. 4—IIc & d).

Fig. 4—III: Draw a pattern of straight lines. With a very sharp knife-point cut straight down into the wood along each line. (fig. 4—IIIa). This cut will prevent too much wood being removed during subsequent cuttings. At a slight distance from these lines, make slanting cuts, trying to make the bottom of these cuts meet. (fig. 4—IIIb). Repeat this on the other side of your original cuts. (fig. 4—IIIc). The result should be an even 'V' notch line. The principle behind this form of cut is illustrated in fig. 4—IIIe.

When you have completed all the lines of your original pattern, you should produce the design shown in fig. 4—IIId. Hold the blade of the paper-knife firmly while you are making all the cuts, and take care to keep your fingers well out of the way of the penknife blade.

Fig. 4—IV: This is a raised design, so the background has to be removed to expose the design. Use a design of straight lines again, such as that shown – a simple cross, but quite effective. Draw the arms of the cross so that the ends reach the sides, or stop at equal distances from them, as in figs. 4—IVa & b.

With a sharp point, cut just outside the lines, this time slanting the cut away from the design. (figs. 4—IVc & d). Very carefully, and with small cuts, remove the background, working from the edge of the wood towards the cuts already made. (fig. 4—IVe). Exercise particular patience here, because this is when one rash cut can completely mar your work. Use your thumb for leverage and to control your penknife. When you have cut away the background to the depth of your first cuts, you may wish to deepen them and cut away more background to make the cross stand higher. It is not advisable to cut away more than about two thirds of the total thickness of the wood, or you might weaken the handle of your paper-knife.

Finish by paring away excess wood right up to the pencil lines, and sandpaper smooth. (fig. 4—IVf & g). A tip about raised designs: when you are cutting, make the cuts slope **away** from the raised part; this makes the carving much stronger than if the cuts were straight down.

DETAILS OF THE PAPER KNIVES IN FIG. 4h.

NOT TO SCALE

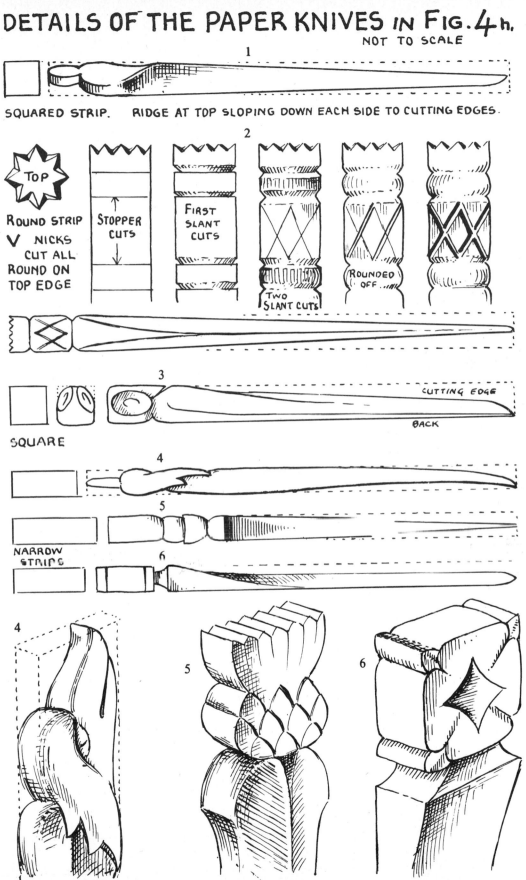

1

SQUARED STRIP.   RIDGE AT TOP SLOPING DOWN EACH SIDE TO CUTTING EDGES.

2

TOP

ROUND STRIP
V NICKS
CUT ALL
ROUND ON
TOP EDGE

STOPPER CUTS

FIRST SLANT CUTS

TWO SLANT CUTS

ROUNDED OFF

3

SQUARE

CUTTING EDGE

BACK

4

5

NARROW STRIPS

6

4

5

6

Now finish off the blade of your paper-knife, and when you are completely satisfied with its shape, use a fine sandpaper to give a smooth, satin feel to it. Where possible, avoid rubbing across the grain as this may cause scratches which are both unsightly and also hard to remove.

As a finishing touch you can then rub a very little linseed oil into the wood; or you can paint the design, or the background. The decision is yours.

Fig. 4h illustrates a few rather more intricately designed paper-knives.

CHAPTER FIVE

Picnic cutlery

It is rather fun using cutlery you have made yourself, and if you take care of it, it will last a long time. So it is worth taking some care over the selection of wood from which to whittle your knife, fork and spoon.

For the knife and fork, select two stout branches about 2cms ($\frac{3}{4}$ ins.) in diameter; the spoon will require a much thicker branch, with a 'Y' fork in it. (fig. 5a). Avoid anything with resin in it. (Check back to Chapter Three for those woods which are resinous.) If you are going to follow the pattern illustrated, you will notice that the handles of each utensil are left uncarved, with the bark still on them, so you will need to select branches accordingly.

KNIFE

Start with a 'stopper' cut right through the wood where you decide the blade and the handle are to meet. Make the cut straight into the wood. (fig. 5b). Then, from the 'blade' side of that cut, make a slanting cut down to the first one, removing a 'V' of wood all round. (fig. 5c). Hold the 'blade' end while you are doing this. Then turn the wood, hold the 'handle' end, and begin to whittle the blade, using the same technique as that used for the paper-knife. (fig. 5d). Remember that your cutlery knife is going to be subjected to much harder work than your paper-knife, so the blade must be stronger. You can achieve this extra strength by leaving the back of the blade fairly thick, and whittling just one cutting edge. An ordinary dinner knife is the model here. Keep it fairly thick as it nears the handle, or it may well snap the first time you use it. The end of the blade should be rounded, not pointed. (fig. 5e & f). Finish off by sandpapering. Don't paint it!

FORK

Start your fork as you did the knife, with a 'V' cut all round. Whittle the prong end, keeping it sturdy and fairly thick. If, when you come to use it, you find it is too thick, you can always go back and whittle away a little more. Retain the whole width of the wood at the prong end, and don't make the shaft too thin. (fig. 5g). When whittling the prongs, cut a small 'V' to begin with, and take only thin slivers from each side in turn, otherwise the fork will split right down the middle. (fig. 5h, i, j). Shape the sides a little, and sandpaper to a point. As you become more experienced you will be able to whittle curved prongs, as shown in figs. 5k & l.

SPOON

The spoon is a different proposition altogether, and will be a real test of your skill. You cut it from the forked branch. Two shapes can be made, one flat, the other more of a ladle shape (fig. 5m & n).

Using your hacksaw, cut off the excess wood and then cut the same 'V' between the handle and shaft as you did for the knife and fork. Shape the stem roughly, and then you are ready for the more difficult part.

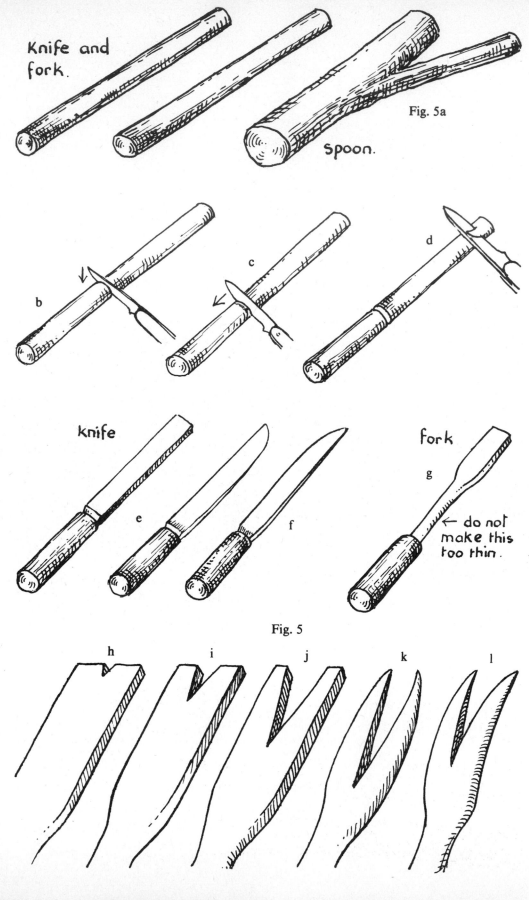

Knife and fork.

Fig. 5a

Spoon.

b

c

d

knife

e

f

fork

g

← do not make this too thin.

Fig. 5

h   i   j   k   l

28

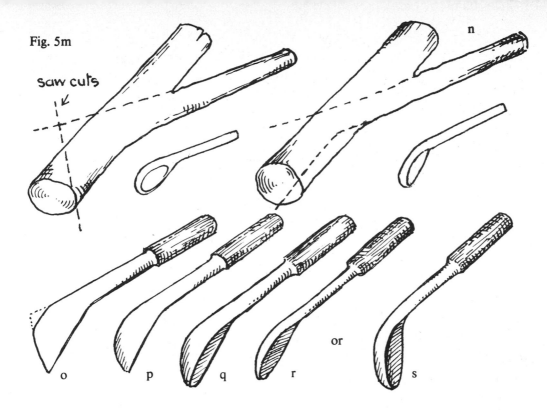

Fig. 5m

saw cuts

n

or

o   p   q   r   s

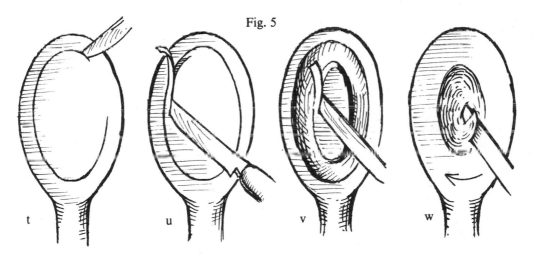

Fig. 5

t   u   v   w

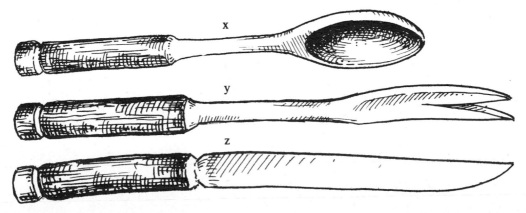

x

y

z

Shape the outside of the bowl as in fig. 5 o, p, q, r or s. The inside of the bowl is the most difficult job, and it will need care and patience to complete successfully.

The first method is to make a deep 'stopper' cut round the bowl, about 1cm. ($\frac{1}{4}$ in.) from the rim. (fig. 5t). Cut a 'V' round the inside of this cut. (fig. 5u). Continue to work round and round the bowl in this manner—making 'stopper' cuts inside the bowl, and working down to them (fig. 5v) until you have hollowed out the centre.

A second method, if you have a good strong sharp knife, is to use the point as a pivot. Start by pressing the point into the middle of the bowl, then, by swinging the knife backwards and forwards, it is possible to gouge out quite a lot of wood. Cut only on the forward movement of the blade, and do not dig too deeply into the wood with the point as it is all too easy to snap off. (fig. 5w). Hold the bowl cupped in one hand and turn it round against the blade, KEEPING YOUR FINGERS OUT OF THE WAY.
(See also Napkin Ring, fig. 6.)

A third way to hollow the bowl is to burn it out with a hot poker. However, this tends to harden the wood, making it more difficult to smooth off afterwards. It can also leave unsightly scorch marks if you are not very careful. The bowl can be finished by sandpapering away any ridges with coarse sandpaper, and smooth with fine grade.

The shaft can now be cut down to the thickness you require, and smoothed off. The handles may be left plain, or with some decoration cut into the bark. (fig. 5f). Remember that you will have to hold your cutlery, so smooth the ends carefully.

A set of finished cutlery is illustrated in fig. 5x, y, z.

CHAPTER SIX

Napkin rings and Scarf rings

Napkin rings and scarf rings are not as difficult to make as they might at first appear. If made well, they can be very effective.

A diameter of about 5cms (2ins) is ideal for the napkin ring; the scarf ring should be slightly smaller.

Select a branch with good bark, and cut from it a piece as long as you want the width of your ring to be. (fig. 6a).

Hold the piece firmly between your thumb and index finger, keeping them well away from the edge. Put the point of the knife into the centre of the wood, and twist it; at the same time, turn the ring against the knife. This swinging movement will cut out wood on the down pressure of the blade, and will make a cone-shaped depression. (fig. 6b & c).

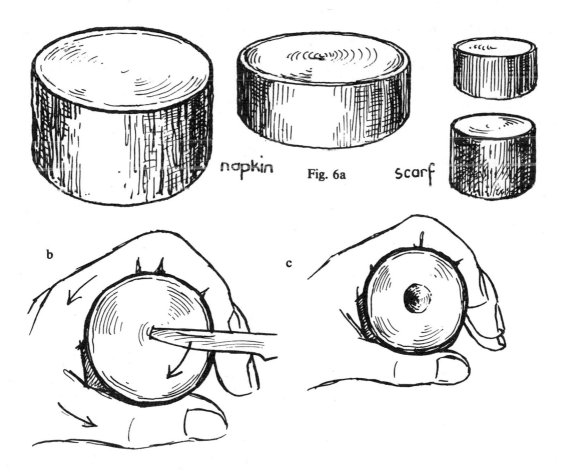

napkin   Fig. 6a   scarf

b

c

Fig. 6

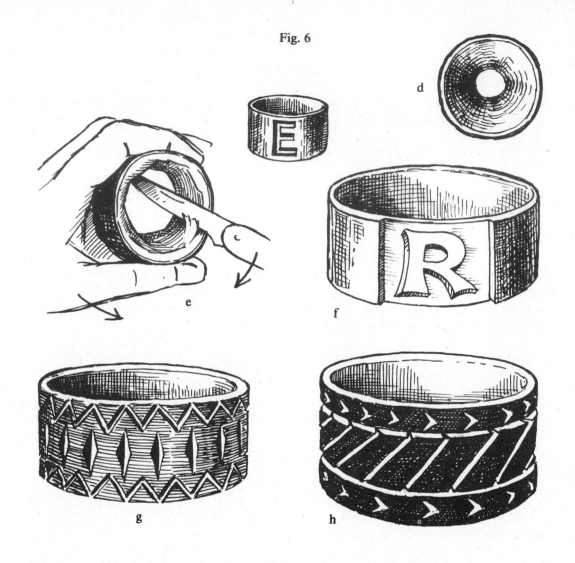

Turn the ring over and do the same on the other side. It is advisable to take a little out of each side in turn rather than try to go straight through the wood from one side.

Your two cone-shaped hollows will eventually meet, leaving you with a hole right through the wood, and thus making a ring. Scoop out more of the wood from the inside, turning the ring continually so that it is of an even thickness all round. Make sure you do not carve out too much wood, or you will be left with nothing but a ring of bark.

With this kind of work, it is essential that the knife be sharp at all times. A blunt blade could easily slip, leaving you with cut fingers.

Sandpaper the inside of the ring as smooth as possible. The outside can be polished—many barks polish up beautifully—or you might prefer to remove the bark and polish up the wood. Finally, you can carve initials or a design on it. (Fig. 6f, g, h, and see also fig. 4–III d).

CHAPTER SEVEN

Animals and Birds

We now leave whittling in kindling wood and small branches and turn to whittling in wood blocks, and larger branches squared off to form blocks. (fig. 7a).

Start with soft wood, and go on to harder and denser woods only after you have gained experience in handling your penknife.

When selecting wood for a project, care must be taken to ensure that the grain of the wood runs in the right direction. For example, if you are going to make a long, thin carving, the grain should run the length of the wood; if it runs across, there is every likelihood that the carving will break in two. (fig. 7b).

Some of the pieces illustrated in this book were whittled from old, well-seasoned wood discarded when alterations were made in an old house. Small blocks were cut from the best pieces and trimmed to size. The rough, dirty and sometimes painted surfaces were cleaned up with coarse sandpaper, then finished off with the finer grades.

Once you have chosen your block, find the centre and draw a line right round it. This is in the depth dimension, and is an aid to making both sides alike. (fig. 7c).

On one of the surfaces draw a simple outline of the animal or bird you propose carving. Use a pencil, as it is much less likely to stain the wood than biro or felt-tip pen. Make the outline fill as much of the surface area as you can, not only because it is a waste of good wood to carve a small piece from a large block, but also because it will save you the job of whittling away large quantities of unwanted wood. (fig. 7d).

Making sure that your penknife is really sharp, whittle away the wood round the pencil outline. Don't try to cut right up to the line at this stage; just concentrate on cutting the block roughly to shape. (fig. 7e).

Once you have the rough shape, you can start to cut right down to the design. (fig. 7f). You will by now have discovered that the grain cuts more easily in one direction than the other. The easy cuts are those made along the grain; cuts across the grain are harder, and result in much slower work.

To finish the simple silhouette shape illustrated, sandpaper down the sharp edges to round them off slightly, then smooth it all with a fine sandpaper. A nicely grained piece of wood will only require a good wax polish to bring out its beauty, and then nothing more need be done to it.

The simple technique described above is that on which almost all carving and whittling is based. So take trouble to get it right, and you will develop your own technique on which you can build your own experience of handling different methods for different types of work.

Before you start on a more detailed carving of a bird or animal, try and find pictures of them taken from different angles – front and side views; from the top, if possible as well.

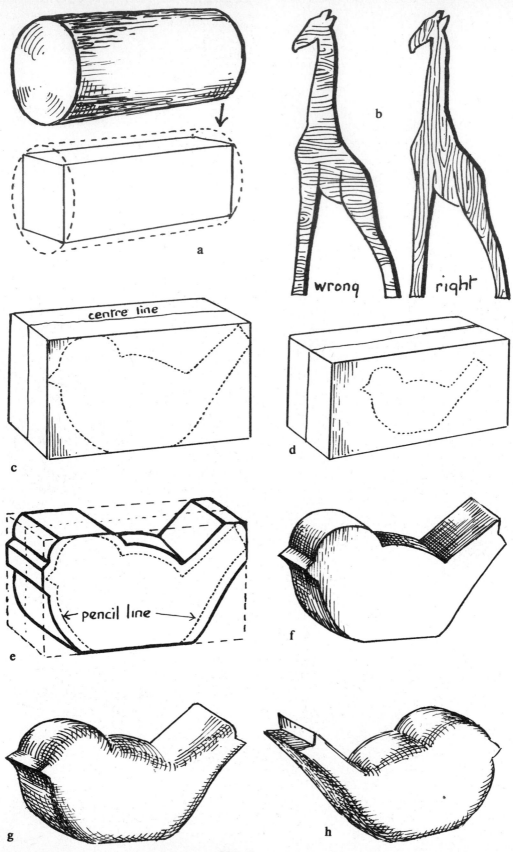

wrong   right

centre line

pencil line

a
b
c
d
e
f
g
h

Fig. 7

i

j   looking down on the top

front   k   back

l

m

n

o

cut deeper here

Fig. 7

Note the width of the body compared to that of the head. Note, too, how the legs are joined to the body, and exactly where they are joined. Compare the length of the limbs to that of the body; study how the neck is set on the body, and how long it is compared to the overall length of the animal or bird.

Keep all these factors in your mind when you start to draw your outline. Make the most of your block of wood by drawing your outline so that the head touches the top and the body touches the sides to begin with. The head, of course, will have to be whittled away on either side later to make it narrower.

As before, we will start off by trying a bird – a widgeon. Draw the centre line all round the block, and outline the bird on one side surface. On the top of the block draw an outline of the bird as if you were looking down on it. On the front, draw the outline of the head, and on the back draw the tail. (fig. 7i, j, k).

Now carry on whittling the rough shape as described above (fig. 7e, f) until your shape looks something like fig. 7l.

Now comes the really interesting part – shaping the bird. As always, remember to turn the wood all the time, and do not try to complete any one part ahead of any other. Keep whittling all round the work, and gradually the whole bird will take shape under your hands.

Whittle the head on each side, and, at the front, on either side of the beak. Round off the shoulders and underpart, and narrow down the hinder parts. (fig. 7n). When you are satisfied with the final shape (fig. 7m), form the eye and the wing feathers. Make 'stopper' cuts by cutting down into the wood on the pencil lines; then, with the point of the knife lying almost flat on the wood, slide the blade towards the 'stopper' cuts to shave off small slivers of wood (fig. 7o). Finally, sandpaper with a fine grade to smooth the surface, then wax or paint. (See also fig. 12).

CHAPTER EIGHT

Adapting from pictures

An ability to draw well is not given to everybody, but there are ways to get round this problem if you are one of those people who do have difficulty in drawing. Whatever you do, don't let an inability to draw stop you from trying to whittle animals, birds, heads and so on.

Remember that the outline is the most important factor; keep it simple, and, to begin with, simplify all the other features until you have built up the confidence to tackle more detailed work.

Whenever you see something that appeals to you, be it in a magazine, a newspaper, or on a card or calendar, put it carefully aside until you feel ready to try it. Then you can trace it, or redraw it to the size you require as explained in fig. 14. There is no need to draw in all the lines from the original; stick to those which will give you the outline and the principal features.

Illustrated are a few carvings, with details of where they were first found.

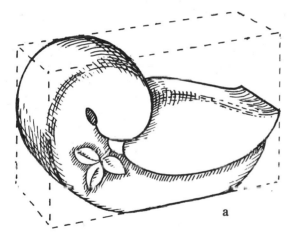

a

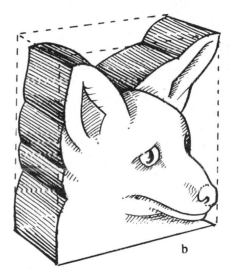

b

c

Fig. 8a, b, c.   Adapted from old Greeting cards.
(b) simply had the body removed.

Fig. 8d, e.   From a book on Nature.

Fig. 8f.   From a catalogue.

Fig. 8g.   From a photograph in a
                    Sunday newspaper.

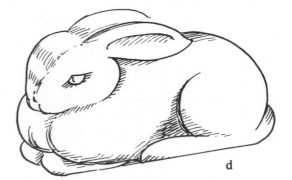

d

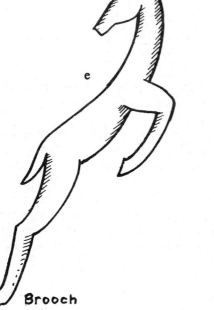

e

Brooch

f

g

Fig. 8

CHAPTER NINE

A variety of things to make from off-cuts

This chapter illustrates a variety of whittled pieces, from a variety of woods, from a variety of sources. Each has a short description and a drawing to explain relevant points. Not all the drawings are to the same scale.

Fig. 9a.   Mouse; tortoise; leaf; owl; beetle; fish. All were whittled from the chips of wood picked up after a tree had been felled. The mouse's ears and tail are leather, and glued on. The owl was left with the rough bark untouched, and the cut face of the chip was carved to form the features.

Fig. 9b.   Dog; hedgehog; ram; bird; leaf. Small pieces, cut from the wood of date, cigar and other boxes. They were made into brooches, with a groove cut out in the back to take a safety pin, which was glued in. The cut was then smoothed over with plastic wood. Some were left plain; others were first sandpapered, and then painted.

Fig. 9c.   Thistles. Two brooches from off-cuts of Malayan teak left over when a floor was being renewed. The wood has a lovely grain, so it was left just polished.

Fig. 9d.   Leaf; snail; rabbit; horse; squirrel; buttons. More off-cuts discarded from a workshop, made into brooches, and buttons. The latter had small screw eyelets for shanks.

Fig. 9e.   Noah; his wife and children; animals. The human figures were cut from an old broom-handle, with the minimum amount of cutting and shaping, and painted. The animals came from a number of odd pieces. In the case of all of these, only the outlines were cut out; the details were painted in.

Fig. 9f.   Four chess sets. These were carved from an old broom-handle, and some squared strips and other scraps from a joiner's shop. Some were whittled very plain in design. One set had painted features. Two have more detail, and were carved in light and dark woods.

Fig. 9g.   These odd creatures were carved from driftwood, ivy stems and burrs from felled trees. The snake needed only to have the head shaped, and a tongue added, made from twisty ivy stem. The cow came from an old branch, with bits sawn off and a burr left for the nose. The cats were made from driftwood; very little detail was added, full use being made from defects in the wood.

Fig. 9h.   Chopsticks and Spurtles were made from dowel rods, and squared rods from a model shop. The chopsticks should be not less than 2cms ($\frac{3}{4}$ins) square; not less than $\frac{1}{2}$cm ($\frac{3}{16}$ins) round, and 30cms. (11ins) in length. Spurtles? What are they? you are probably asking. They are what the Scots use for stirring their porridge instead of a wooden spoon. These were made from dowel rods roughly 2cms. ($\frac{3}{4}$ins) in diameter, and 30cms (11ins) long. lightly carved and left plain. For hints on the designs, see figs. 4 & 7.

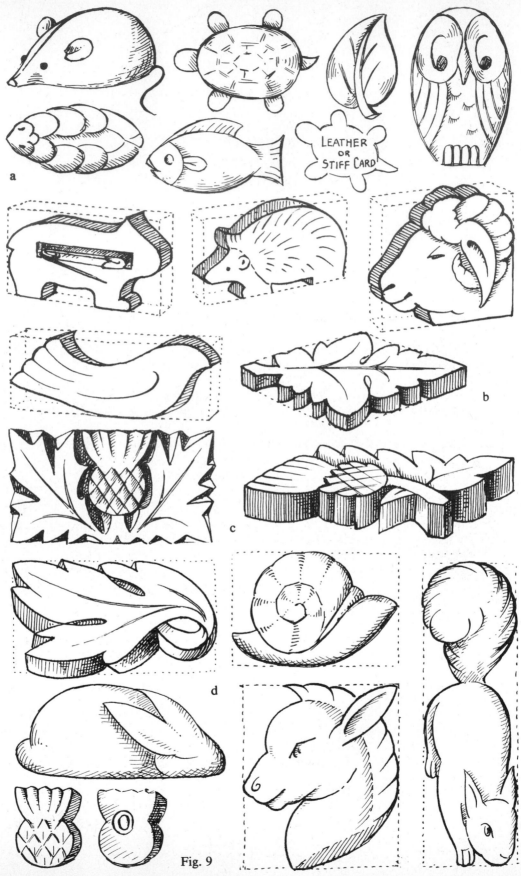

LEATHER OR STIFF CARD

a

b

c

d

Fig. 9

40

Fig. 9e

Fig. 9f

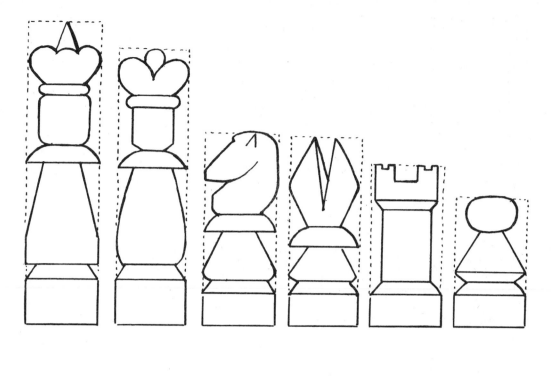

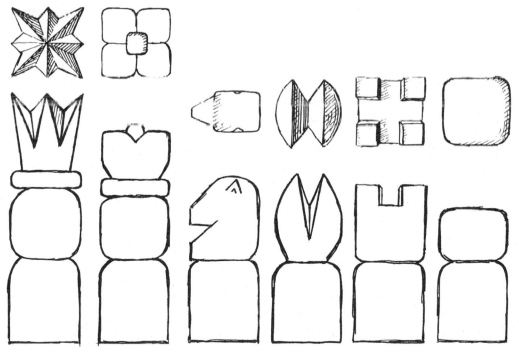

Fig. 9f

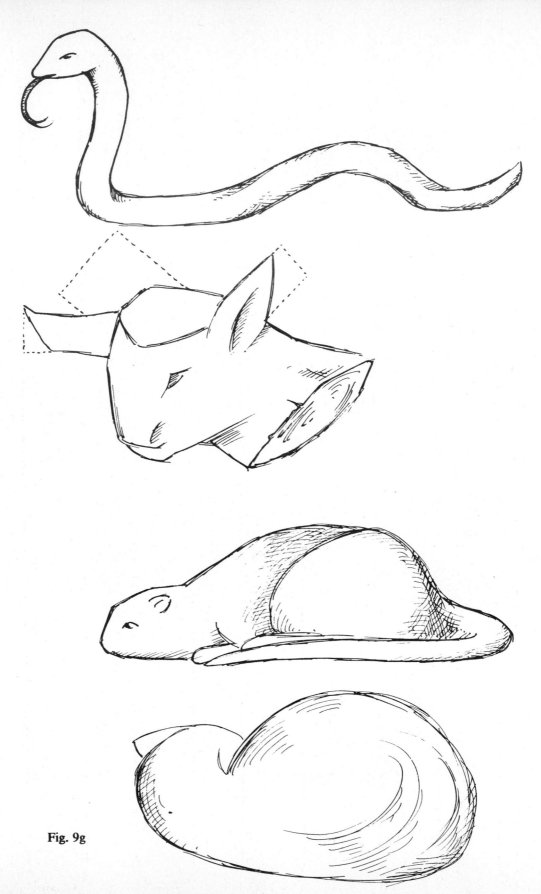

Fig. 9g

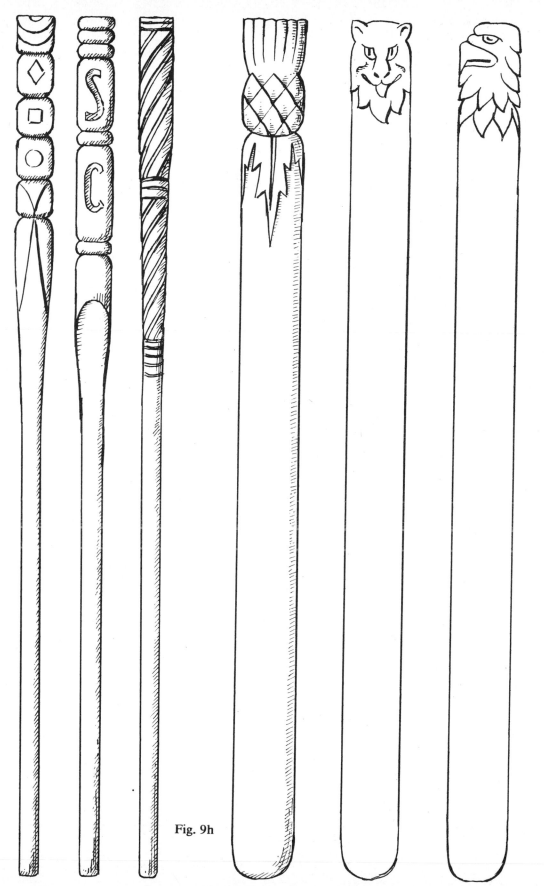

Fig. 9h

45

CHAPTER TEN

Walking Sticks

Although walking sticks are usually straight, there is no reason why they should be. When you are out in the fields and woods, you may come across cut or gale-broken wood. Look for anything you may think suitable, provided it will be strong enough to stand the use to which it will be put. You may find a stick with a slight curve, or one with side branches, which when trimmed, may leave interesting knobs and circles. Another may have a side branch just asking to be whittled into a head for the handgrip, or two branches to make a thumb-stick. (fig. 10).

Hazel branches are usually quite straight; birch makes good sticks, and hawthorn has interesting shapes. With or without the bark, designs or motifs should be cut, to give a personal touch.

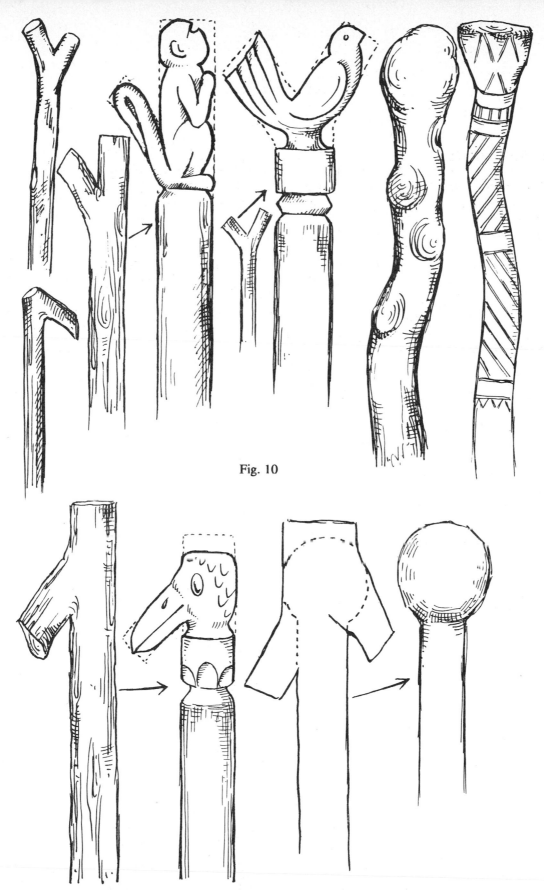

Fig. 10

CHAPTER ELEVEN

Totem Poles and Symbols

Totem Poles are objects on which you can really let yourself go, whittling and designing as you go along, making use of all the knots and blemishes, to bring some queer beast into being! The totem can be any or all patterns: queer figures; animals; birds; symbols which have a meaning only to you, and, of course, woodcraft designs. They may be of any size, though you will probably find that those illustrated are large enough to start with.

These were whittled from:

a.   A foot-long birch branch
b.   A strip of old flooring
c.   A lime branch two feet long
d & e.   From old picture frames with rebate and moulding smoothed off.

To add extra features, like beaks, noses, wings or bases, cut grooves and slots as illustrated, and glue on the extra items. When completed, poles can be left plain, or you can stain or paint them.

Going into a little more detail about each:

Fig. 11a.   The rich, red-brown bark was left on; the whittled design made a pleasing, contrasting effect, so it was left plain, but polished.

b.   The pinewood flooring was polished to bring out its very interesting grain.

c.   The lime bark was peeling, so the branch was stripped, revealing interesting markings due to the ravages of insects, so this was left plain.

d.   This was plain pine wood, painted in bright colours and varnished.

e.   This was mahogany, left plain and varnished.

(a) and (b) tell a brief story about the person who carved them.

Fig. 11f & g.   Here are a few symbols suitable for carving or for painting on your sticks and totems.

Monday: The Moon Goddess. Symbol: a half-moon.
Tuesday: Tyr, God of Battle. Symbol: Sword and shield.
Wednesday: Woden (or Odin) had two ravens sitting on his shoulders.
Thursday: Thor, God of Thunder. Symbol: a hammer.
Friday: Frigga, Goddess of Spring, fertility and love.
Saturday: Saturn's day.
Sunday: Balder, the Sun God. Symbol: the Sun.

The symbols for months given here are just suggestions. You may have other symbols more suitable for the area in which you live. You may, also, like to depict your hobby, or other activities. In fact, the ideas are endless so go ahead and think up a range of your own.

a

b

c

arm

beak

d

e

wing

beak

Fig. 11

49

A FEW SYMBOLS TO CARVE ON YOUR WALKING·STICKS OR TOTEM POLES.

 EARTH

 DAY

NIGHT

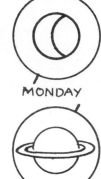 MONDAY

 TUESDAY

 WEDNESDAY

THURSDAY

FRIDAY

SATURDAY

 SUNDAY

JANUARY

FEBRUARY

MARCH

APRIL

MAY

 JUNE

 JULY

AUGUST

SEPTEMBER

 OCTOBER

 NOVEMBER

 DECEMBER

 JANUARY

 FEBRUARY

 MARCH

 APRIL

 MAY

 JUNE

JULY

AUGUST

 SEPTEMBER

 OCTOBER

 NOVEMBER

 DECEMBER

 SEPTEMBER

 OCTOBER

 NOVEMBER

 DECEMBER

Fig. 11f

SPRING SUMMER AUTUMN WINTER

WINDY RAINING SUNNY STORM

TOTEM ON 'NICK' NAMES

ARIES TAURUS GEMINI CANCER LEO VIRGO

LIBRA SCORPIO SAGITTARIUS CAPRICORNUS AQUARIUS PISCES

Fig. 11g

51

CHAPTER TWELVE

Soap carving

Once you have mastered the techniques for carving, you might like to try another medium other than wood. Soap is just such an alternative. Use 'household' soap as opposed to 'toilet' soap, as the latter tends to be too soft. The colour of the cheaper soap can also be a asset, the yellow and green looking very attractive when carved.

The only tools you will require are: a penknife; a cloth to clean the blade; tracing paper; a pencil; ballpoint pen, and, lastly, a box in which to catch the chips. Don't ignore that last item; if soap chips are left on the floor, they might be trodden on, and as they can be very slippery, a nasty accident might be the result.

Start by scraping the trade name off the soap, and level it to a uniform smoothness. Place the soap on the tracing paper and trace round its outline. Within this outline draw the bird, animal or other shape to be carved, just as you did for wood carving. Again, as with wood, try and fill as much of the space as you can, letting the drawing touch the outside line whenever possible. This elephant is a quite simple shape with which to start. (fig. 12a).

Place your drawing on the soap and go over it with a ballpoint pen, using only as much pressure as is needed to make a mark on the soap. (A knitting needle or any object with a strong point will do as well as a ballpoint.) Remove the tracing paper, and go over the line where necessary.

Turn the paper and repeat the process on the other side of the soap. Make sure that you turn the **paper,** or your elephant will be facing different ways.

Cut away the surplus soap in small chips, working across the whole width of the soap. Put your box on the floor between your legs to catch any chips, which you will then be able to melt down and reuse. Don't carve right up to the line at this stage; leave that for later. (fig. 12c). This shows what should be carved away, and fig. 12d shows that material carved away.

Keep the blade of your knife clean, wiping it as soon as any soap clings to it. When all the surplus soap has been removed, you can start cutting right up to the line. (fig. 12d).

When you have finished, you can start putting in the details. With just the tip of the knife, and very little pressure, cut a 'stopper' line round the ears. (fig. 12e). Wipe the knife, and lay it flat on the soap; slowly and gently slide it towards the stopper cut, getting deeper the closer you get to the cut. Then, with a stroking motion, slice away slivers of soap. (fig. 12f). This will make the ear stand out from the body. Now do the eye.

Fig. 12g shows the underside. Lightly round off the square edge a little, and lastly rub the surface with the cloth to remove loose chips. Polish by rubbing gently in the palm of the hand and with your fingers.

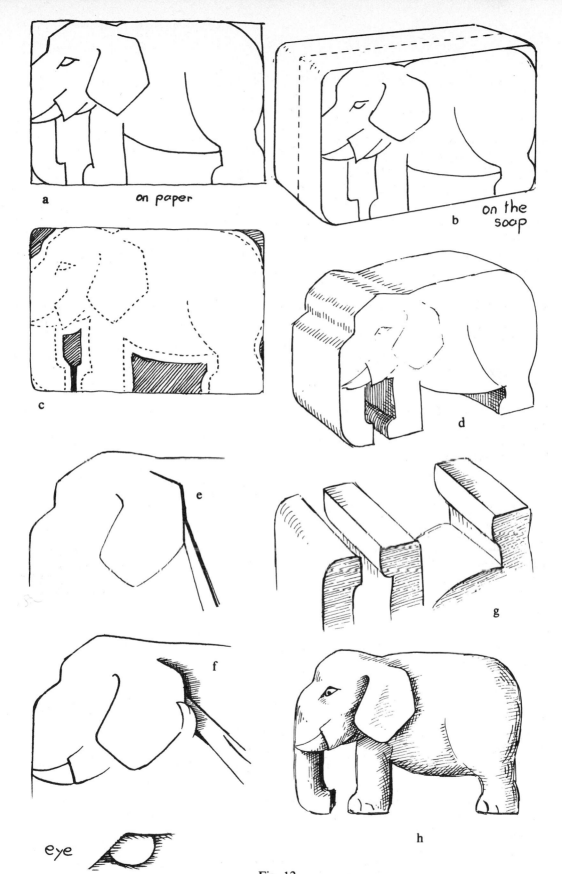

a   on paper

b   on the soap

c

d

e

f

g

h

eye

Fig. 12

Fig. 12 i-p shows a rabbit, worked step-by-step as was the elephant.

i: The outline on tracing paper
j: Surplus soap cut away, almost to the drawn outline
k: The rabbit, cut up to the outline
l: Modelling the inside of the ear
m & n: Modelling the leg and features
o: Squared edges rounded off
p: One step further, with a little more modelling attempted. The head has been shaped, and the divide between the ears. A little has been removed from each side of the feet.

The tortoise

This is a shade more difficult than the rabbit, but interesting to try.

Fig. 12q: Top and side views, showing surplus soap cut away, the cutting under the shell, the rounding of the tummy and the shaping of the top of the shell.

Fig. 12r: Here the cuts have been deepened, to shape the head, tail, and feet, and the scales on the shell.

Fig. 12s: The final cutting and shaping.

Fig. 12t: Front and back views. Very little detail, with everything kept solid, but the result is obviously a tortoise!

i

j

k

l

m

n

o

p

Fig. 12

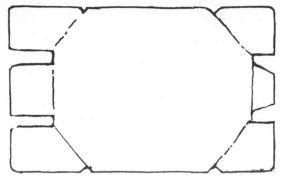

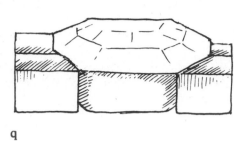
q

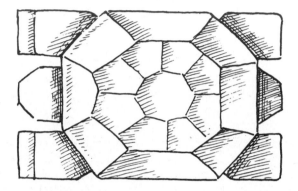

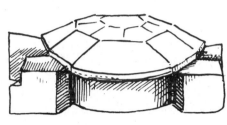
r

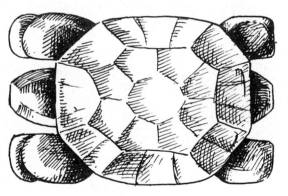

s

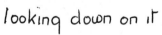
looking down on it

side views

t

front

back

Fig. 12

56

CHAPTER THIRTEEN

Plaster Carving

The technique for plaster carving is very similar to that used for soap carving. Perhaps the greatest difference is that as plaster is harder, but more brittle than soap, it must be scraped rather than cut.

You can carve a plaster block of any size or shape; choose a mould which suits the object you wish to carve. It can be round; square; oval; deep; shallow – in fact, any shape you wish. Almost any container will do as a mould, be it a match-box tray, tin lid, cardboard container or plastic cup. The only condition is that it must be able to hold a semi-viscous liquid. (fig. 13a).

The best medium to use is Plaster of Paris, which can be bought from most chemists or Drysalters. You can buy modelling plaster from Art Shops as an alternative. Whichever you use, make up the plaster exactly according to the instructions; but there are a few general rules which apply to most similar products.

Don't add water to powder. Start with a little water in a bowl, and add powder, a spoonful at a time, stirring gently to avoid forming bubbles in the mixture, until all the water is used up. You will learn by experience both how much to mix, and also the correct consistency for the mixture. If in doubt about the quantity to make, always err on the generous side. (fig. 13b). Don't use a spoon for both adding powder and mixing; the wet spoon, if put into your bag of powder, will spoil the powder, so use a stick for stirring.

Pour your mixture into the selected mould, smooth off and level the top, and allow it to set. Setting takes about 15 minutes for a small mould. Remove the mould and allow the mixture to set and dry off completely. (fig. 13c)

While it is setting, assemble the tools you will be using:

1. A sharp knife
2. Tracing paper
3. Pencil
4. Very fine sandpaper
5. A box, for chips

Draw the selected outline on tracing paper (fig. 13d), turn the paper over and go over the outline again with a soft pencil, on the other side of the paper. This will act like carbon paper, and is used to transfer the image later. (fig. 13e).

Make sure that the surface of the plaster block is smooth – sandpaper it if necessary – then lay the design on it, right side up, and go over the outline with a hard pencil, a ballpoint pen or similar hard point, to leave an impression of the soft pencil on the plaster.

The actual carving is the same as for soap, except that you will find it easier to scrape rather than shave the plaster. This medium blunts a knife very quickly, so frequent sharpening is unavoidable.

Fig. 13f The pig with all surplus plaster removed and the bare outline left.

Fig. 13g, h, i These show the modelling of the various parts.

The finished product can be painted, varnished or kept plain. Water colour paint stirred into the plaster when mixing can give an all-through colour; pink, in fact, was used for the pig which then required no further painting.

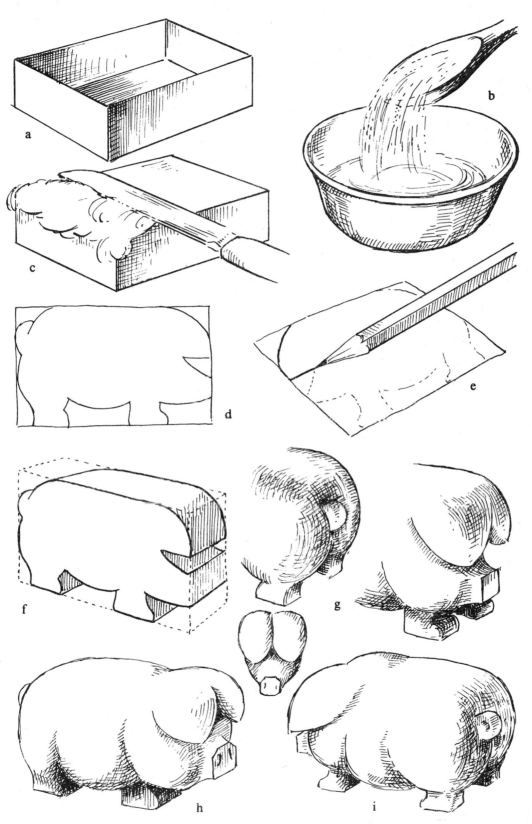

Fig. 13

CHAPTER FOURTEEN

How to reduce or enlarge a picture for copying

Fig. 14a, b, c, d show an easy way to copy a picture, to make it either larger or smaller. (If you want it the same size, then tracing will suffice.)

If the design which you want to copy is on something that you do not want defaced, then you will have to start by making a tracing and using the tracing as your model.

Divide the picture or tracing into squares of equal size. (fig. 14a). This is the pattern from which you will work.

TO REDUCE A DRAWING

On another piece of tracing paper, draw a grid of squares smaller in proportion to the first as the size you require is in proportion to the model. That is to say, if you want the drawing to be half as wide and half as long, then make the squares half as big as those on the pattern. Remember, though, that halving the square size will produce a drawing one quarter the size of the original.

If you have problems working out the proportions, it is best to draw the size of the picture that you want, and then divide that into as many equal squares as the pattern is divided into. All the squares should be numbered, as in Fig. 14a, b. Working from square to square, copy the larger picture on to your smaller, keeping the proportions the same in both.

TO ENLARGE A DRAWING

The principles for enlarging are the same as for reducing. The only difference is that the squares of the pattern are copied into larger, not smaller squares, the latter square having been already drawn to the required size.

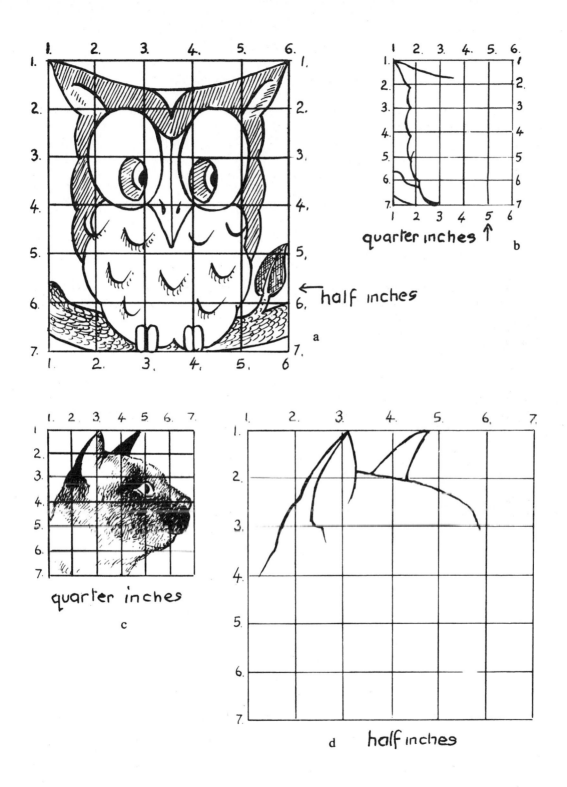

quarter inches ↑ b

← half inches

a

quarter inches

c

 half inches

d

Fig. 14

CHAPTER FIFTEEN

Extra tools

If you have followed all the steps in this book, you will by now be quite an experienced carver and whittler, and you may feel that you would like to try more ambitious work. At this stage, you may well need better tools than those you have been using up to now, so here are a few suggestions about what you may need.

a. If you have a knife with a broken blade, don't throw it away; instead, grind and sharpen it into a SKEW knife (fig. 15a). These can be very handy for awkward corners.

b. An extra penknife is always useful, if only because a change of grip can ease your hand. It can also be ground to a different point for delicate work. (fig. 15b).

c. A sheath-knife or jack-knife is a help in whittling away excess wood, and it will ease the load on your lighter blades. But it must be very sharp to avoid spoiling the work. (fig. 15c).

If you can afford a wood-carver's GOUGE you will find carving such things as spoons much easier.

d. You can use an old grapefruit knife, with its turned-up end made really sharp, for spoon carving. The blade's lower part can be bound with string both to give a better hold and also to protect the fingers. (fig. 15d).

e. Small files of different shapes are always useful. (fig. 15e).

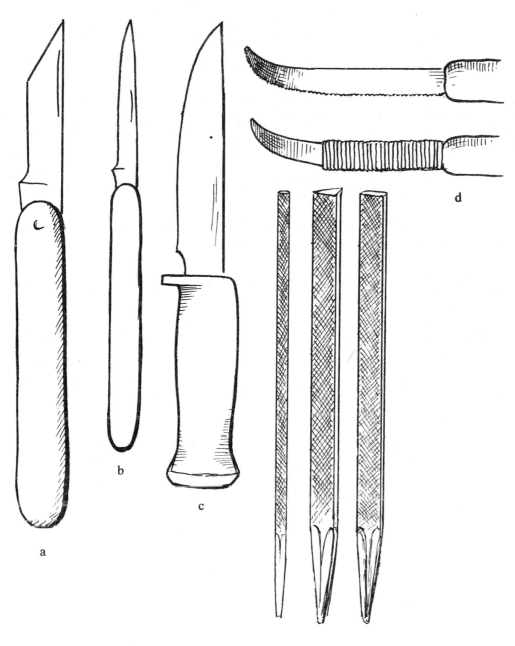

Fig. 15